FEATHERED FRIENDS

CUCKOOS

Kim Thompson

NorwoodHouse Press

Cataloging-in-Publication Data

Names: Thompson, Kim.
Title: Cuckoos / Kim Thompson.
Description: Buffalo, NY : Norwood House Press, 2027. | Series: Feathered friends | Includes glossary and index.
Identifiers: ISBN 9781978580442 (pbk.) | ISBN 9781978580459 (library bound) | ISBN 9781978580466 (ebook)
Subjects: LCSH: Cuckoos--Juvenile literature. | Cuckoos--Life cycles--Juvenile literature.
Classification: LCC QL696.C83 T548 2027 | DDC 598.74--dc23

Published in 2027 by
Norwood House Press
2544 Clinton Street
Buffalo, NY 14224

Designer: Rhea Magaros
Editor: Tricia Hoffman

Photo credits: Cover, p.1 Piotr Krzeslak/Shutterstock.com; p.5 Edwin Godinho/Shutterstock.com; p.6 Agami Photo Agency/Shutterstock.com; p.7 Dennis W Donohue/Shutterstock.com; p.9 avilledorsa/Shutterstock.com; p.10 Peter Garrity/Shutterstock.com; p.13 Vishnevskiy Vasily/Shutterstock.com; p.14 Vishnevskiy Vasily/Shutterstock.com; p.17 Karyne Wee/Shutterstock.com; p.18 Jesus Giraldo Gutierrez/Shutterstock.com; p.19 BirdsEyeViewPhotography23/Shutterstock.com; p.21 WildMedia/Shutterstock.com;

Printed in the United States of America

TABLE OF CONTENTS

What Do Cuckoos Look Like?

Cuckoos are our feathered friends. There are more than 100 cuckoo **species**. These birds are shy. If you are lucky enough to glimpse one, you'll see a brownish-gray and white bird with a curved **beak**.

Cuckoos have long legs and tails. Some have spots, stripes, or patches of bright color.

The smallest cuckoos are about the length of a dollar bill. Roadrunners and other large cuckoos can be as long as a skateboard.

Where Do Cuckoos Live?

Cuckoos live in **tropical** and **temperate** areas around the world. Black-billed cuckoos and yellow-billed cuckoos live in much of the United States. Mangrove cuckoos are found in Florida.

mangrove cuckoo

Most cuckoos live deep in forests. They hide in trees and stay very still. You may hear them but not see them!

How Do Cuckoos Grow Up?

Male and female yellow-billed cuckoos work together to build a nest and keep eggs warm. It takes less than three weeks for babies to **hatch**, grow feathers, and learn to fly.

Many cuckoos are **brood parasites**. They lay their eggs in the nests of other birds. The **foster parents** get tricked into caring for the cuckoo babies after they hatch.

Some cuckoo mothers lay more than 20 eggs, all in different nests!

What Do Cuckoos Eat?

Cuckoos eat insects. They love to gobble **caterpillars**! Cuckoos help forests by eating insects that can harm trees, such as tent caterpillars.

What Sounds Do Cuckoos Make?

The common cuckoo lives in Europe. Its call sounds like its name. The cuckoo clock was named for this bird.

Yellow-billed and black-billed cuckoos make knocking sounds, especially before storms. Some people call them "rain crows."

What Funny Things Can Cuckoos Do?

Cuckoos that hatch in the nests of other birds can be larger than their foster parents. Warblers and other little birds struggle to feed the big, hungry babies!

GLOSSARY

beak (beek): the horny, pointed jaw of a bird; bird bill

brood parasites (brood PAR-uh-sites): birds that lay their eggs in the nests of birds of different species and allow the foster parents to care for their young

caterpillars (KAT-ur-pil-urz): butterflies in a worm-like larval stage of life

foster parents (FAWS-tur PAIR-uhnts): people who raise a child who are not the child's biological parents

hatch (hach): to break out of an egg to be born

species (SPEE-sheez): groups of living things that are alike and can reproduce together

temperate (TEM-pur-it): having temperatures that are rarely very high or very low

tropical (TRAH-pi-kuhl): near or having to do with the hot and rainy area near Earth's equator

THINKING QUESTIONS

1. What colors are a cuckoo's feathers?
2. What cuckoo species live in the United States?
3. What is a cuckoo's favorite meal?
4. What does it mean to be a brood parasite?
5. How did the cuckoo clock get its name?

INDEX

ABOUT THE AUTHOR

Kim Thompson is a writer from Columbus, Ohio. She has written many books for kids. Lots of birds come to her backyard feeder. Her favorites are the showy red cardinals, tiny bright goldfinches, and waddling mallard ducks. Her two cats watch from the window.